CELEBRATING THE FAMILY NAME OF HICKS

Celebrating the Family Name of Hicks

Walter the Educator

Silent King Books
a WhichHead Entertainment Imprint

Copyright © 2024 by Walter the Educator

All rights reserved. No part of this book may be reproduced in any manner whatsoever without written permission except in the case of brief quotations embodied in critical articles and reviews.

First Printing, 2024

Disclaimer

This book is a literary work; the story is not about specific persons, locations, situations, and/or circumstances unless mentioned in a historical context. Any resemblance to real persons, locations, situations, and/or circumstances is coincidental. This book is for entertainment and informational purposes only. The author and publisher offer this information without warranties expressed or implied. No matter the grounds, neither the author nor the publisher will be accountable for any losses, injuries, or other damages caused by the reader's use of this book. The use of this book acknowledges an understanding and acceptance of this disclaimer.

Celebrating the Family Name of Hicks is a memory book that belongs to the Celebrating Family Name Book Series by Walter the Educator. Collect them all and more books at WaltertheEducator.com

USE THE EXTRA SPACE TO DOCUMENT YOUR FAMILY MEMORIES THROUGHOUT THE YEARS

HICKS

The name of Hicks is strong and sure, like oak trees standing tall,

Celebrating the Family Name of

Hicks

Through changing winds and seasons wild, they never bend or fall.

With roots that dig deep in the earth, and branches reaching high,

The Hicks name rises with the sun, and soars into the sky.

From humble lands to distant shores, their story has been told,

A tale of grit and courage bright, of hearts both brave and bold.

They walk with honor in their stride, with wisdom in their hands,

The Hicks name shapes the paths of life, across both seas and lands.

Their journey started long ago, when pioneers set sail,

Through every trial, storm, and fight, they did not bow or fail.

In every generation, Hicks have forged a path anew,

With vision sharp and minds alive, they've always followed through.

A family born of dreamers, yet grounded in their way,

They build the future day by day, from stones of yesterday.

The Hicks name stands for more than just a name passed down in time,

It's perseverance in the storm, and joy in life's climb.

Celebrating the Family Name of

Hicks

In towns where people gather close, the Hicks have always known

That family's more than just a word—it's every seed they've sown.

With hands that work and hearts that care, they build, protect, and guide,

For in the strength of love they've shared, the Hicks name does abide.

They've worn the hats of many roles—of farmers, teachers, friends,

Of builders shaping worlds anew, where hope and courage blend.

Through fields of green or city streets, wherever life has led,

The Hicks name finds a way to thrive, on paths both paved and tread.

And while they hold tradition dear, they also chase the new,

With open hearts and curious minds, they always push on through.

For Hicks are never ones to shy from dreams that dare to fly,

Celebrating the Family Name of

Hicks

They balance roots deep in the earth with wings that touch the sky.

Their laughter is like summer rain, refreshing every soul,

Their kindness shines through darkened times, to make the broken whole.

The Hicks name carries joy and light, through every step they take,

A symbol of the lives they've touched, the bonds they never break.

Yet it's in quiet moments too, that Hicks find what is true

In family gathered close at heart, in skies of endless blue.

They cherish simple, sacred things, the warmth of home, a friend,

For in those timeless treasures lies the strength that will not end.

Celebrating the Family Name of

Hicks

Through every season, every turn, the Hicks name stands its ground,

With feet that walk through shifting tides, and eyes on what's profound.

Their legacy is not just built on battles they have won,

But on the love that fills their hearts and shines like morning sun.

ABOUT THE CREATOR

Walter the Educator is one of the pseudonyms for Walter Anderson. Formally educated in Chemistry, Business, and Education, he is an educator, an author, a diverse entrepreneur, and he is the son of a disabled war veteran. "Walter the Educator" shares his time between educating and creating. He holds interests and owns several creative projects that entertain, enlighten, enhance, and educate, hoping to inspire and motivate you. Follow, find new works, and stay up to date with Walter the Educator™ at WaltertheEducator.com

Milton Keynes UK
Ingram Content Group UK Ltd.
UKHW020047181024
449757UK00011B/556